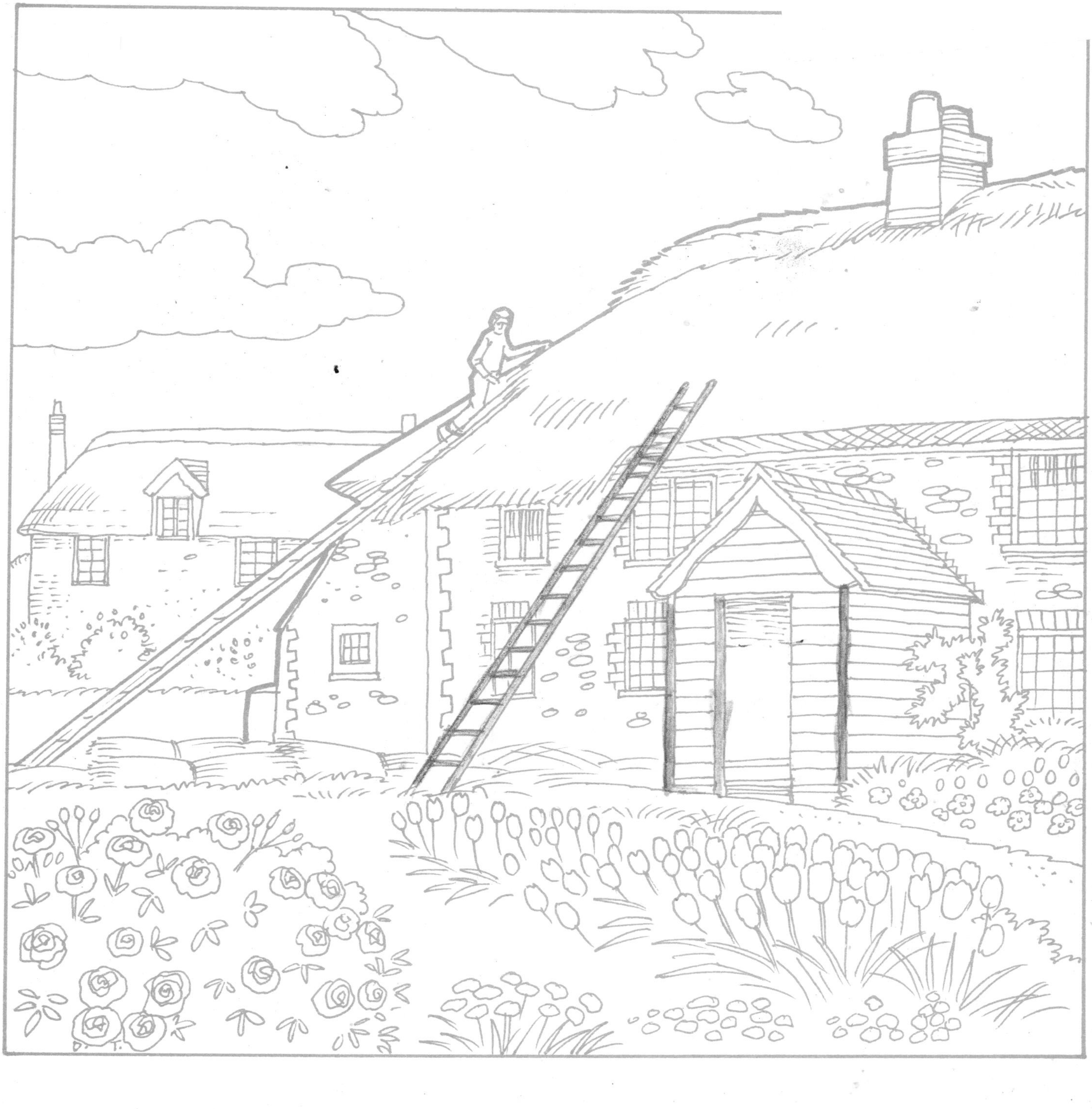

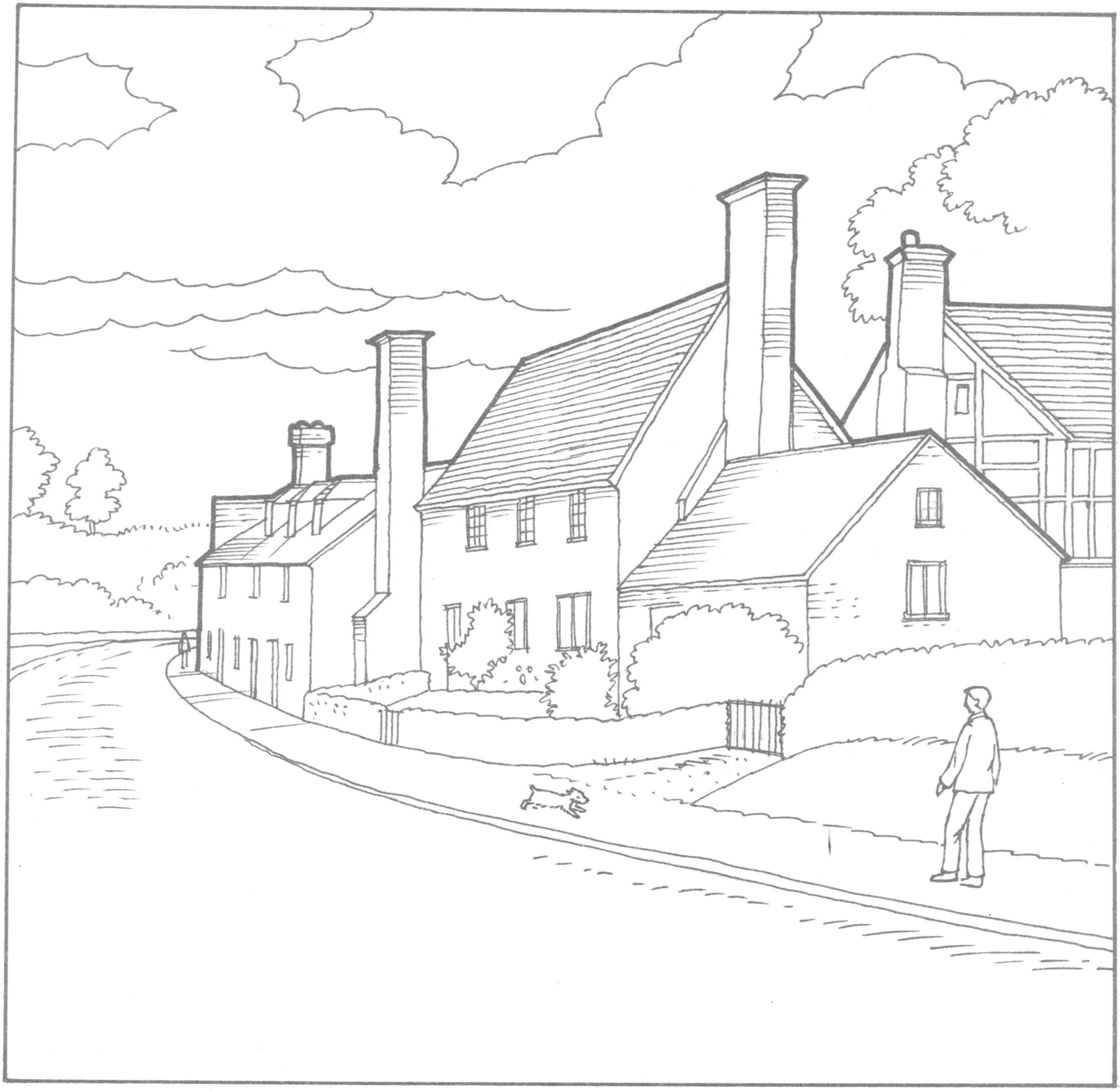

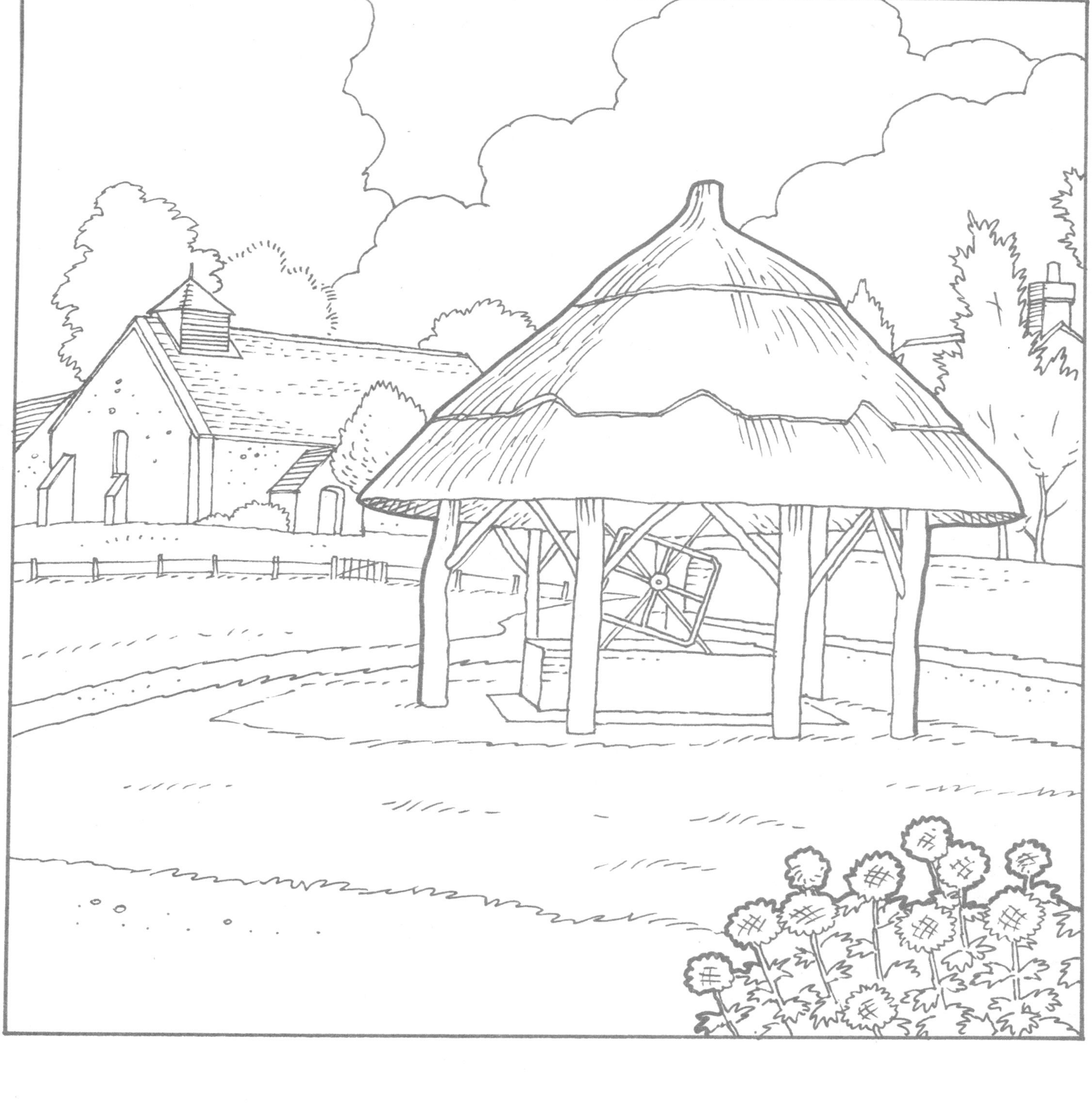

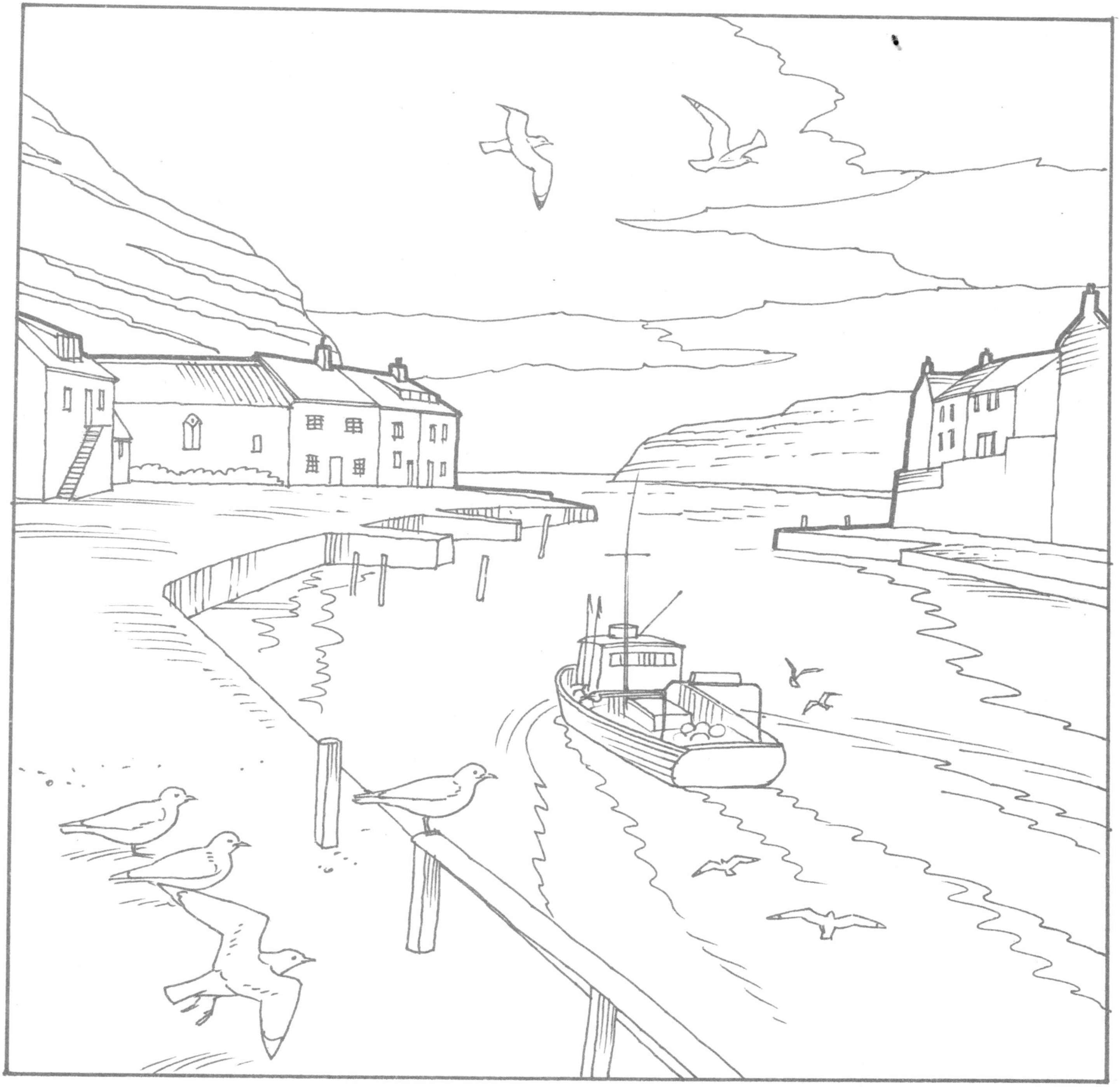

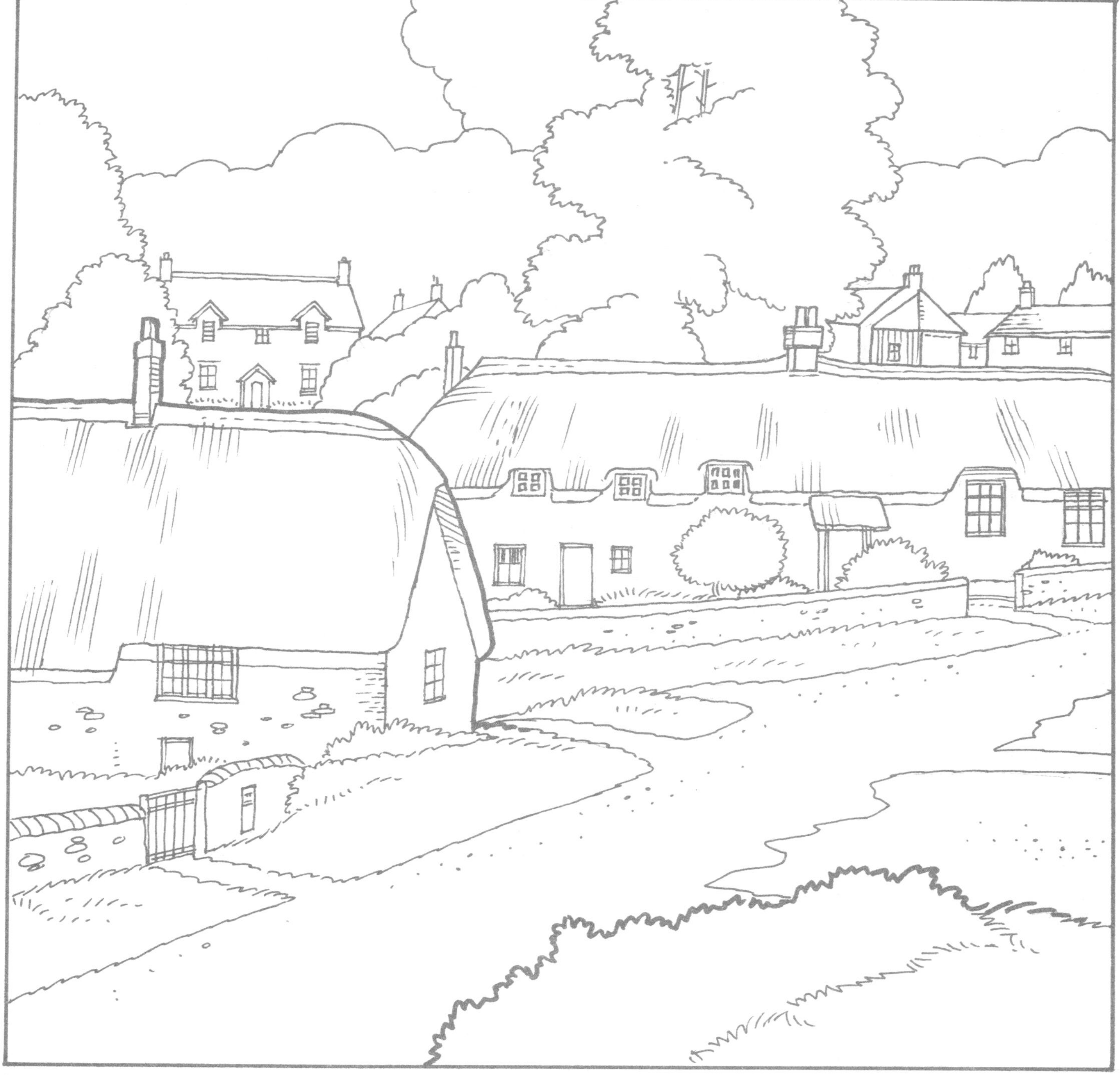

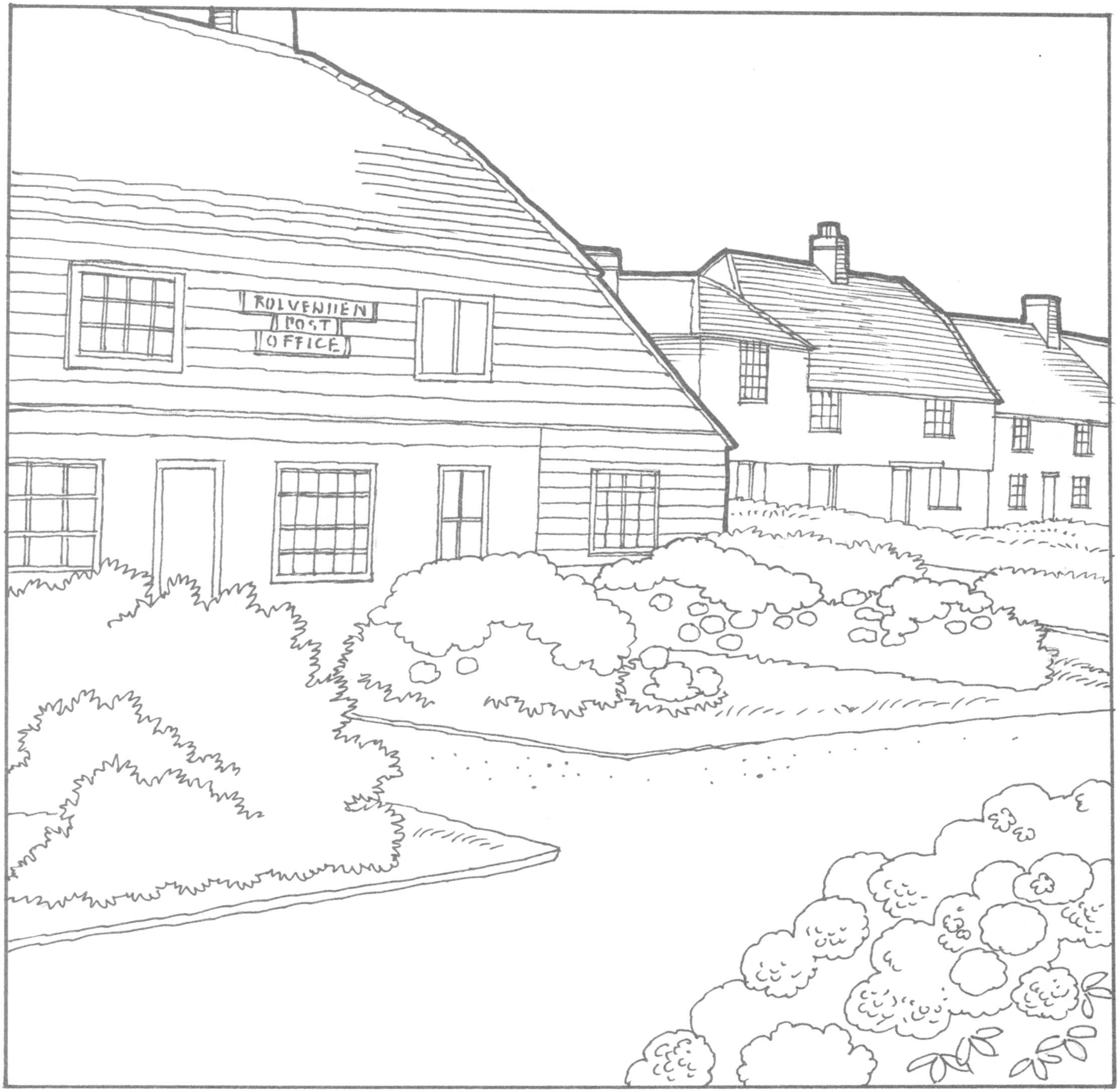
ROLVENDEN
POST
OFFICE

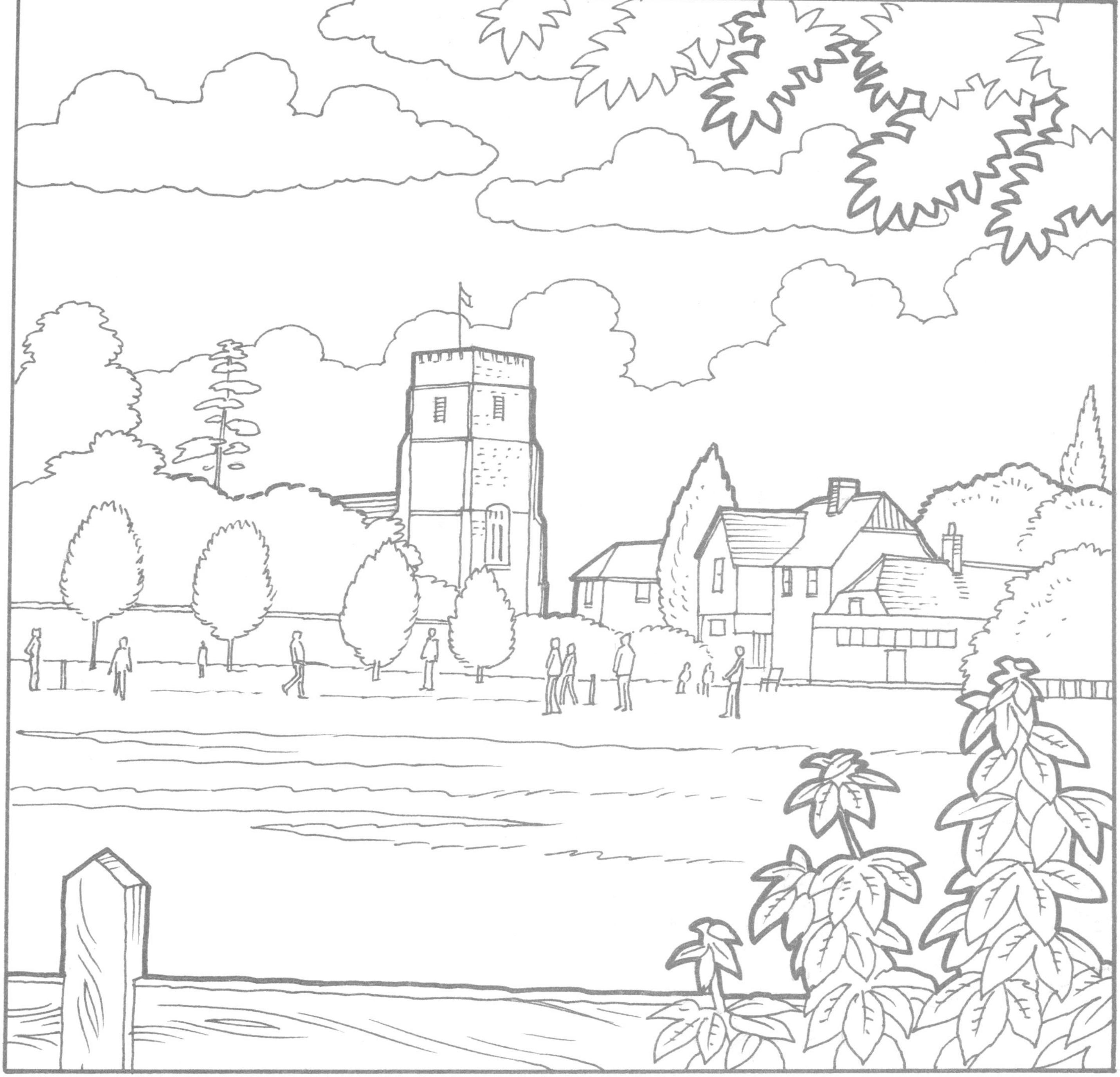

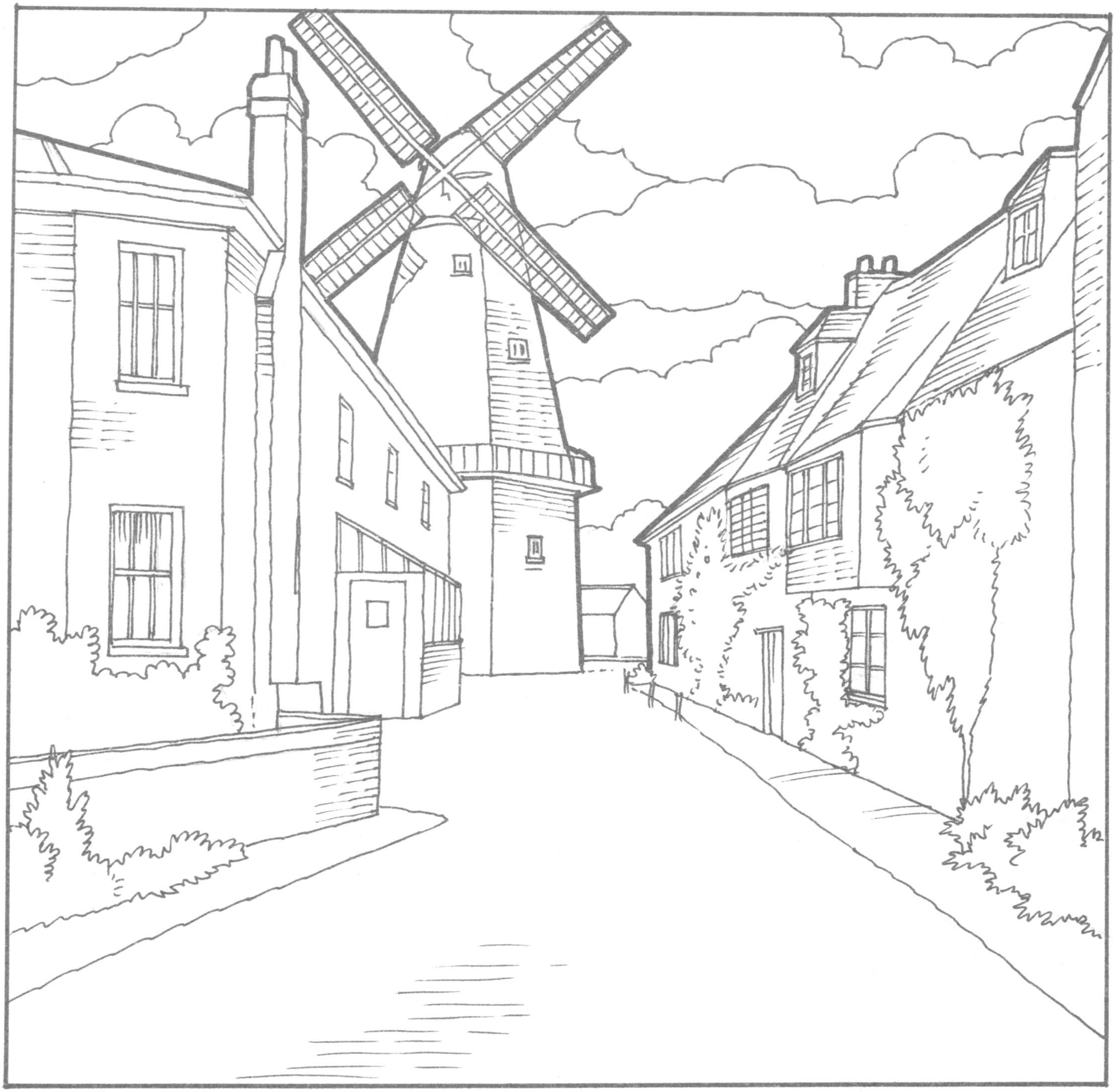

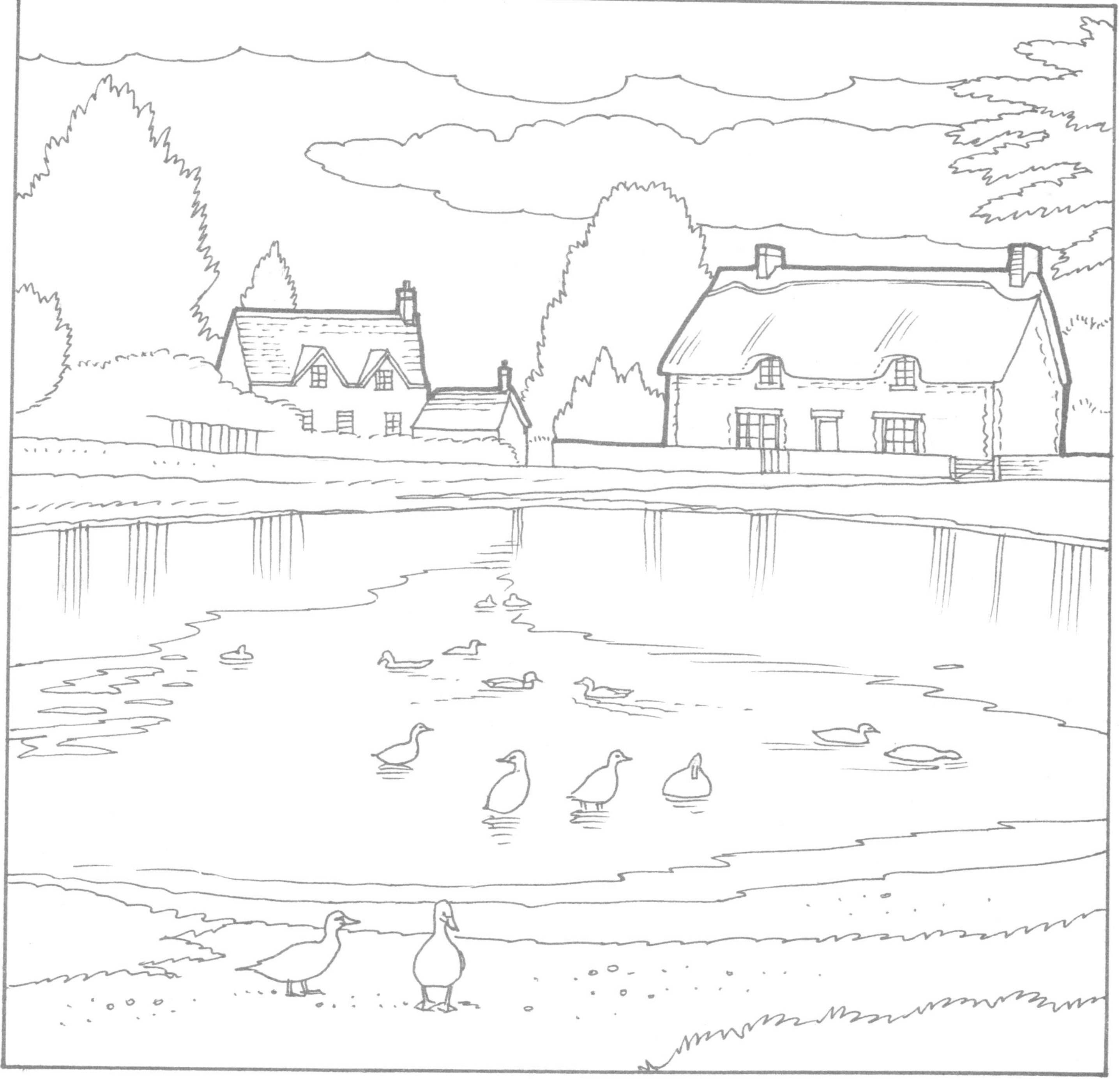

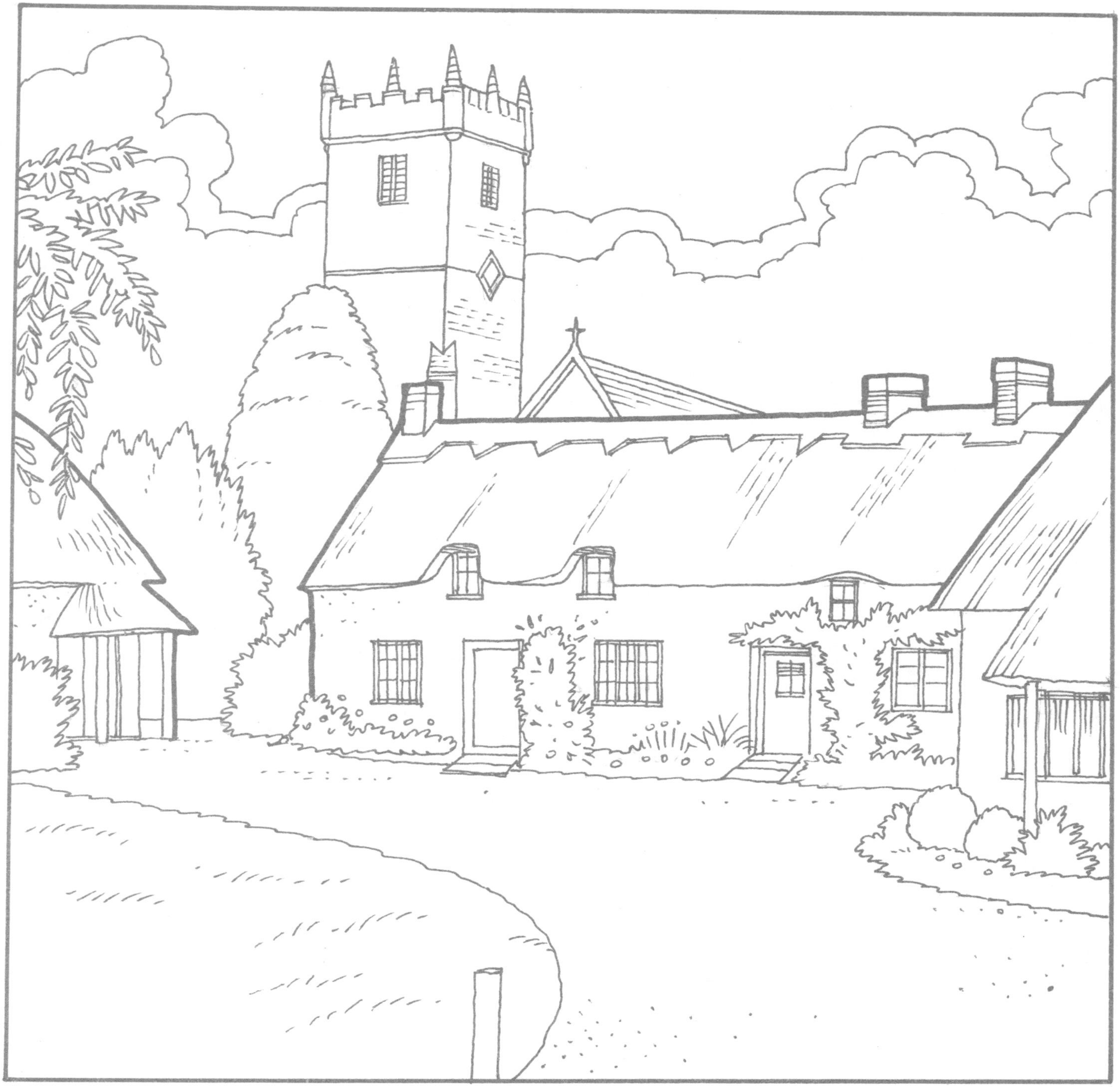

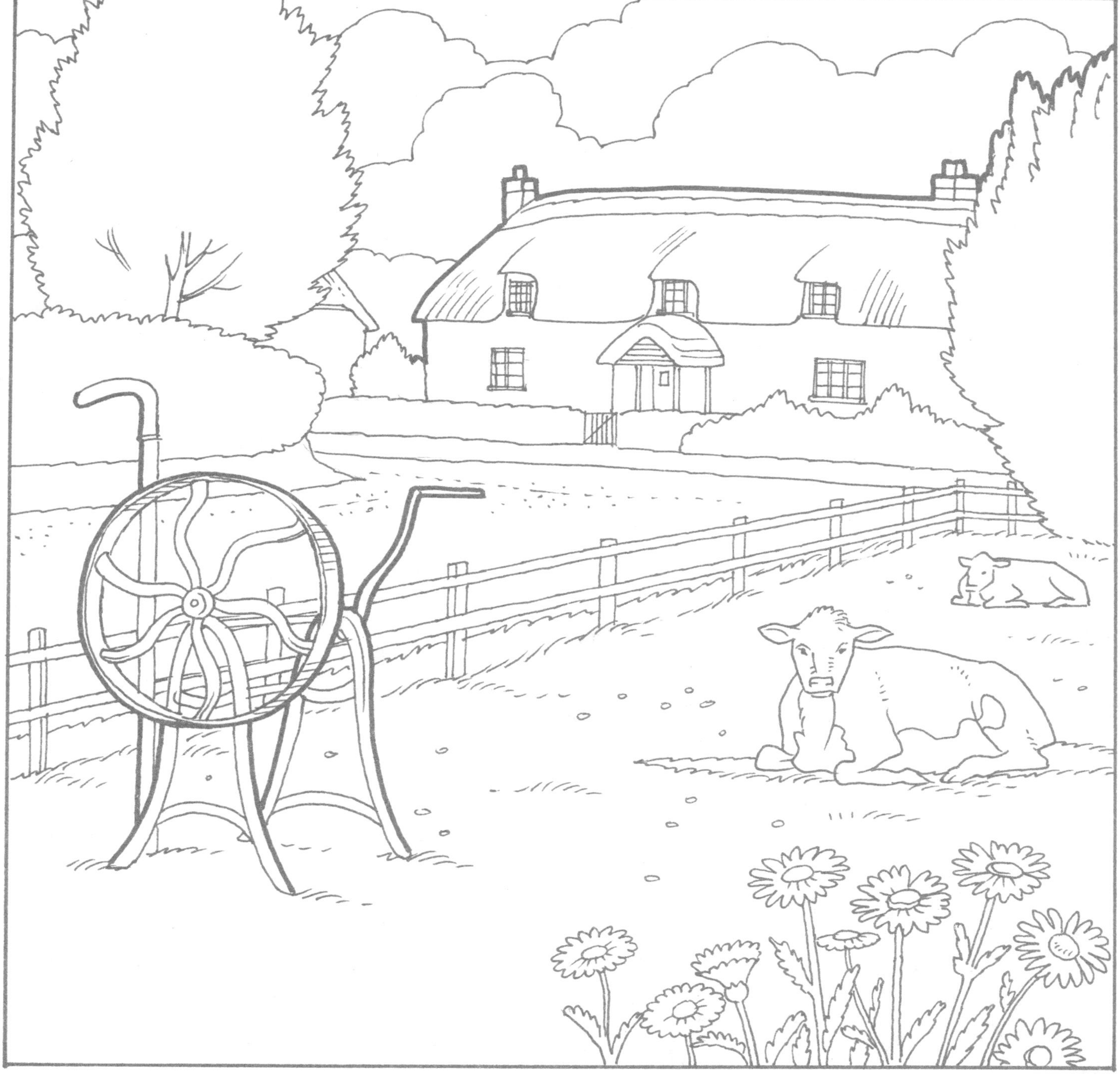

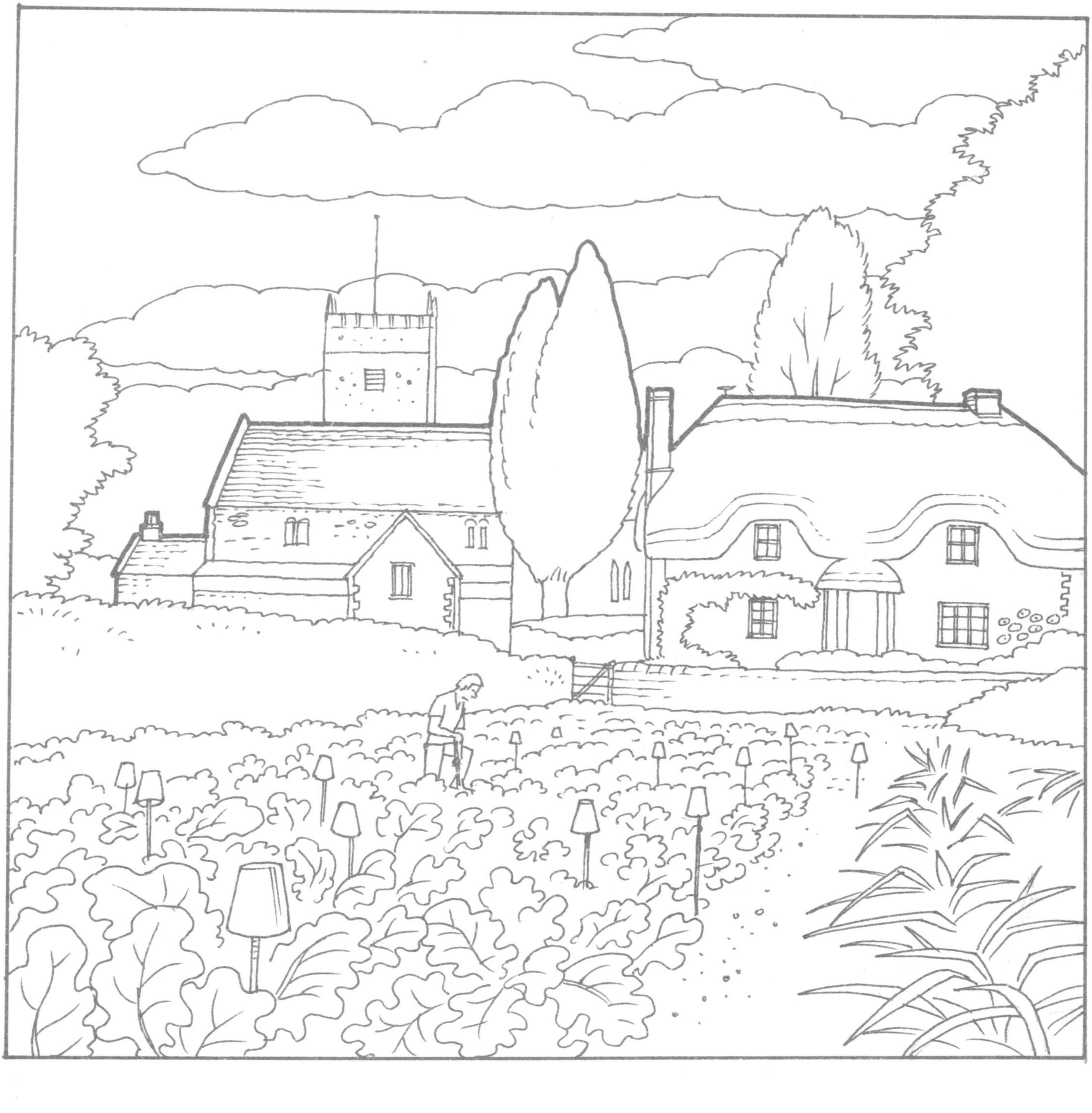

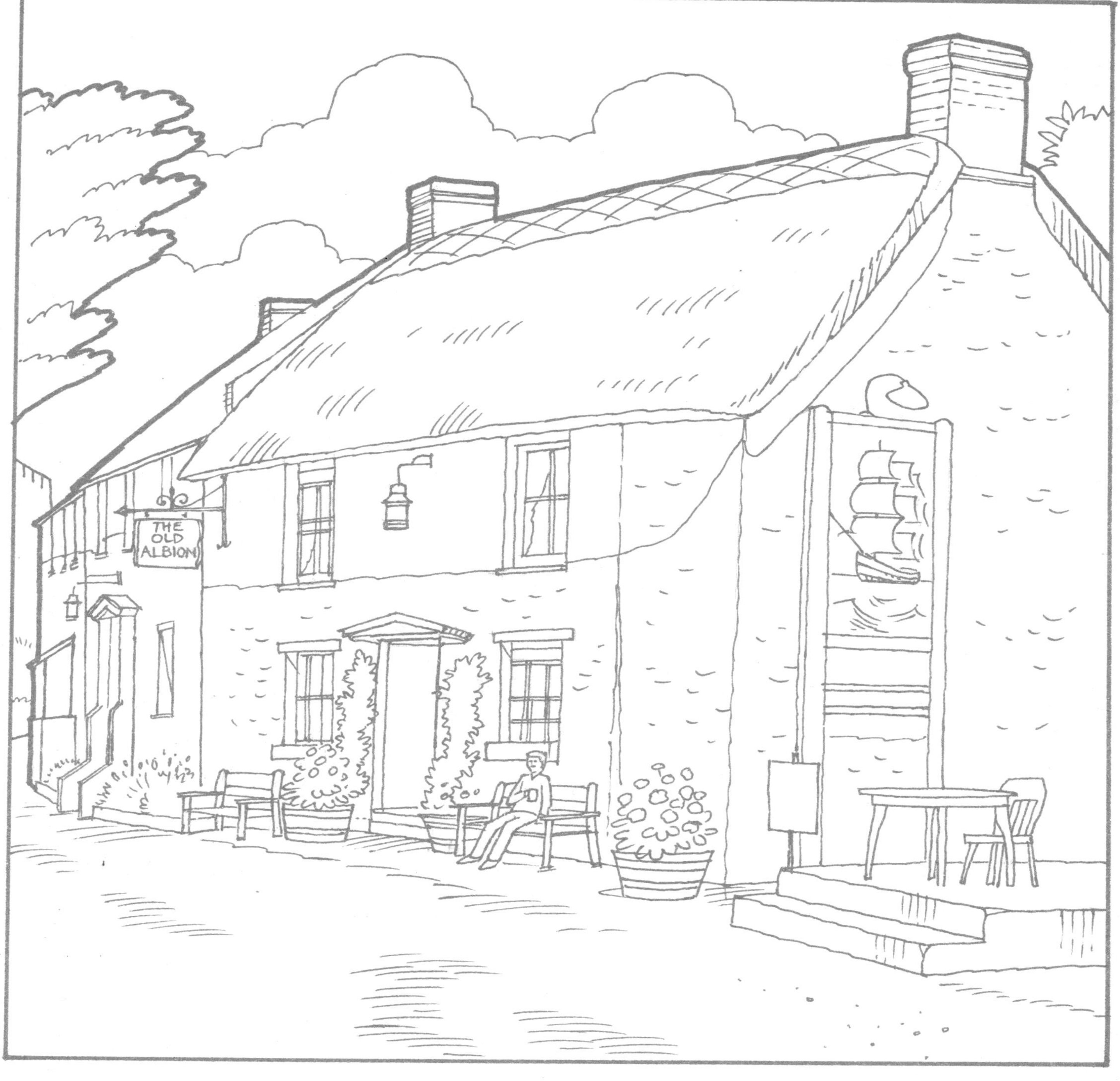
THE OLD ALBION

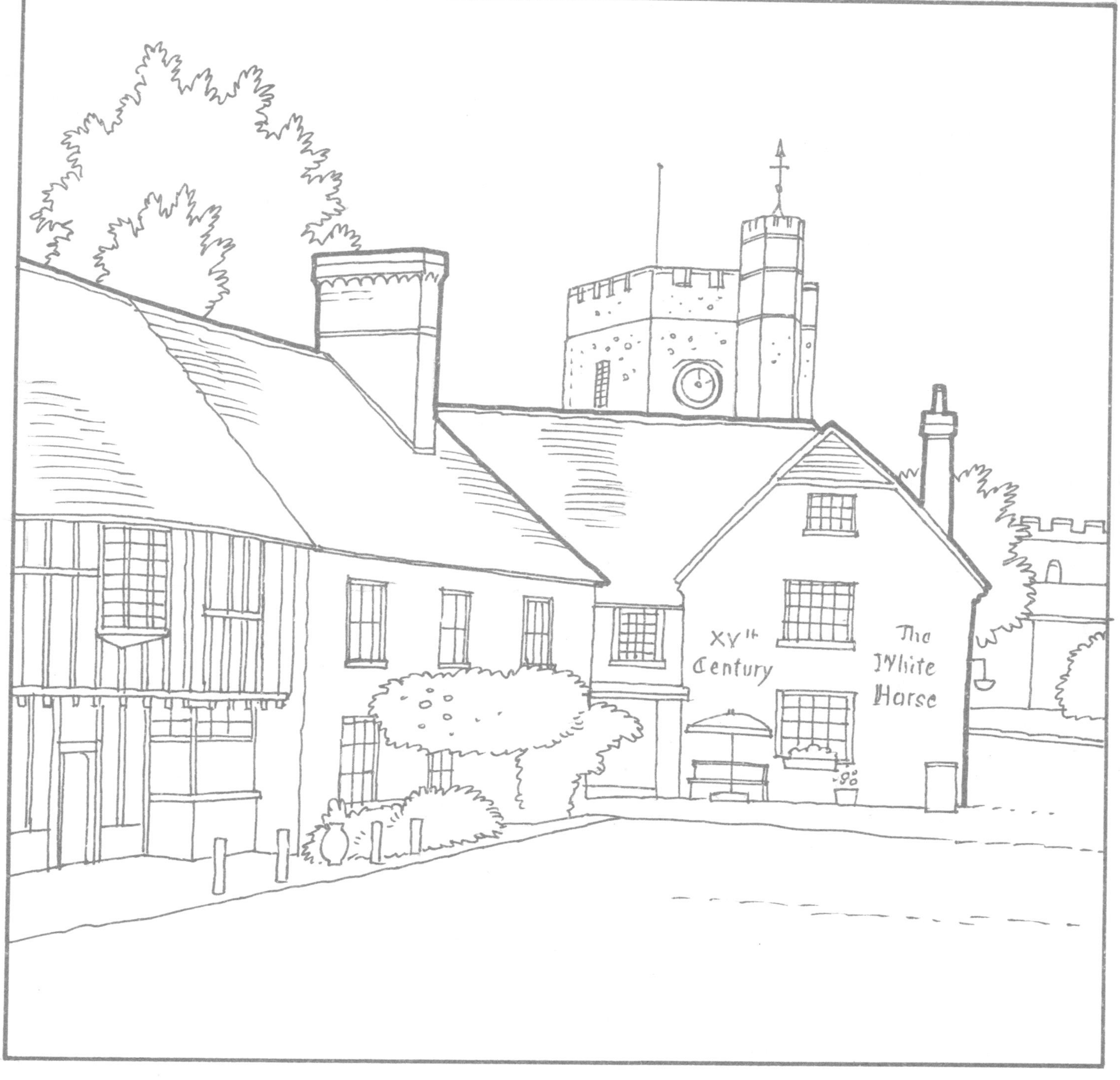
XVth Century
The White Horse

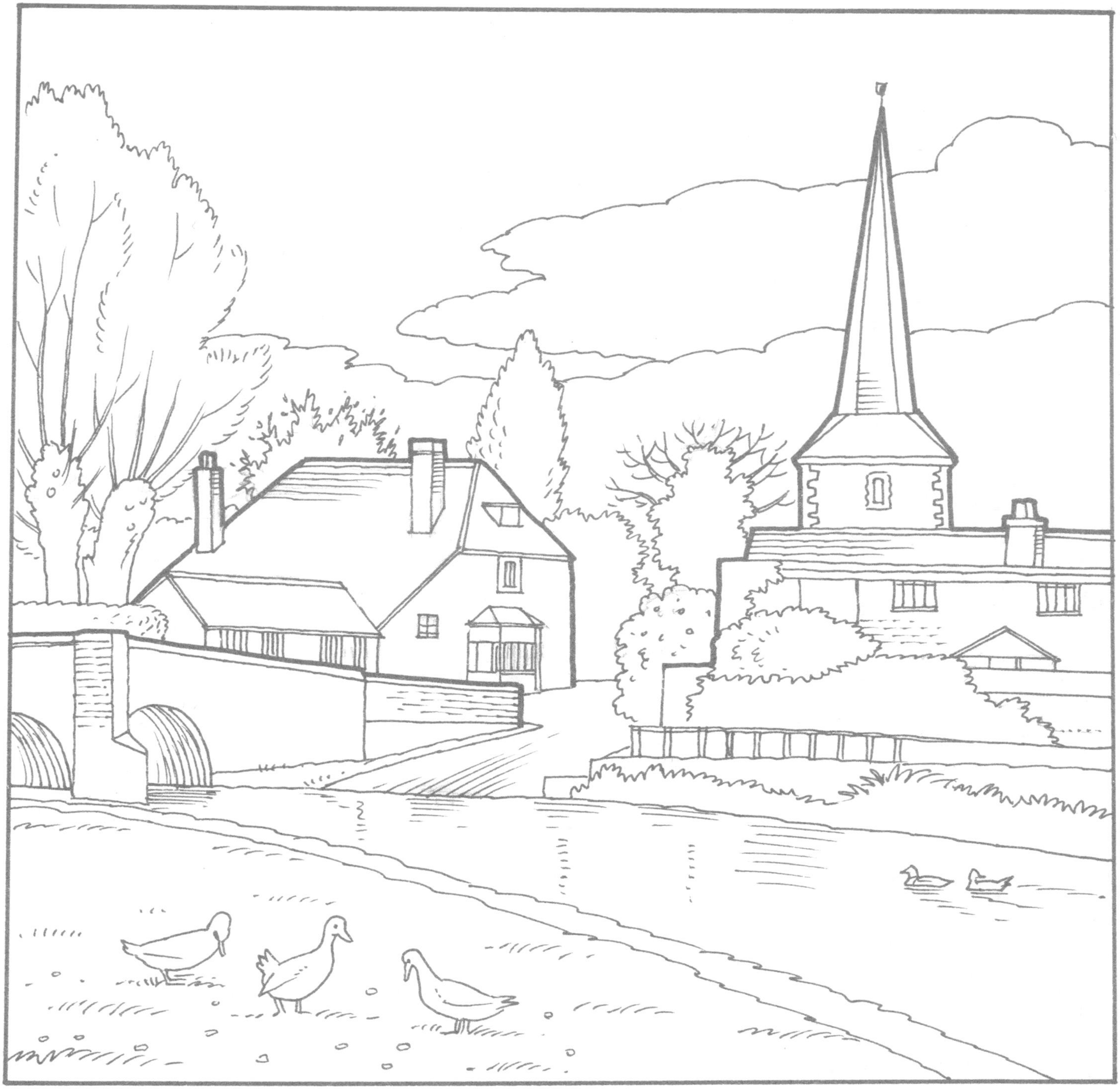

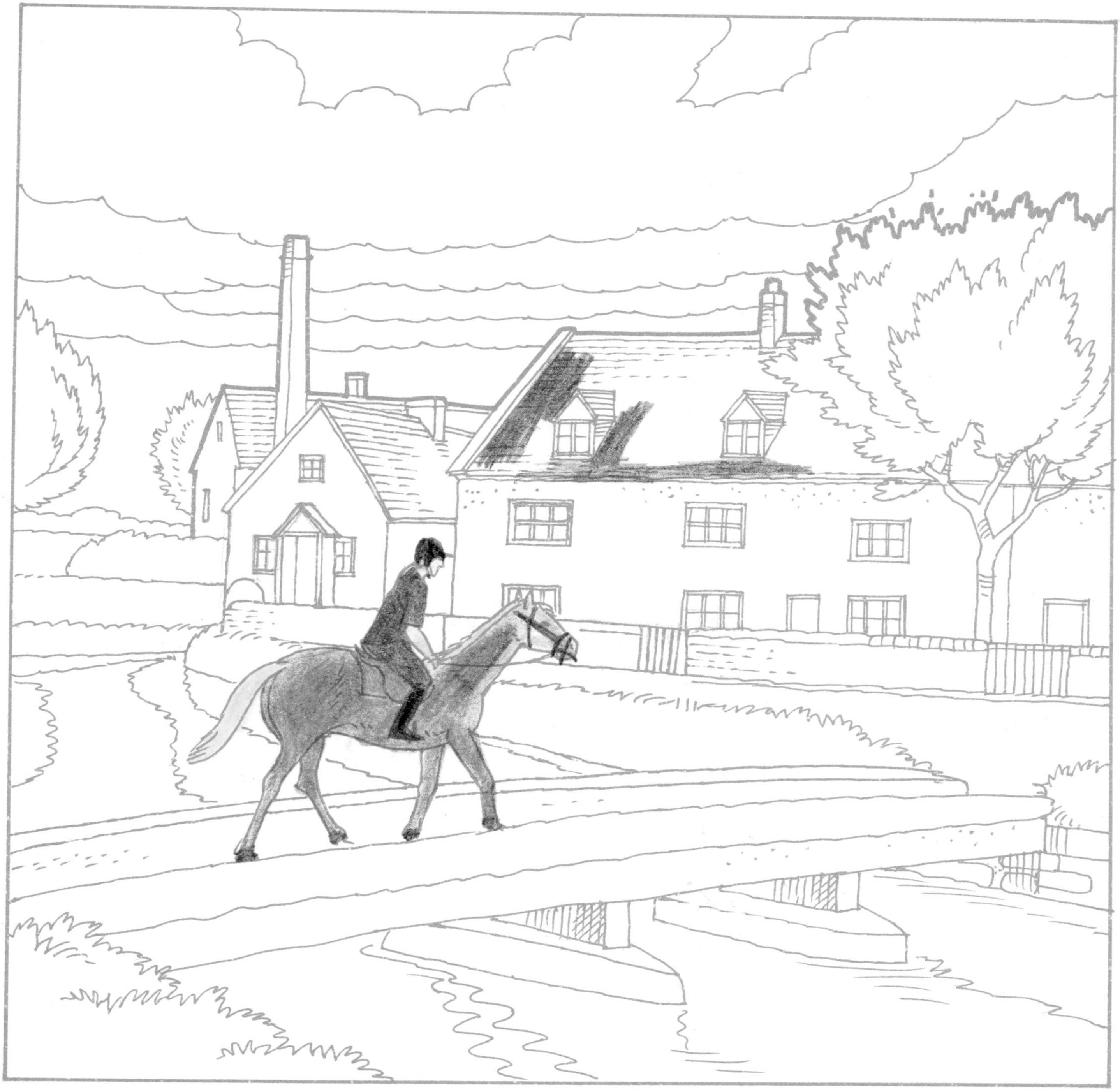

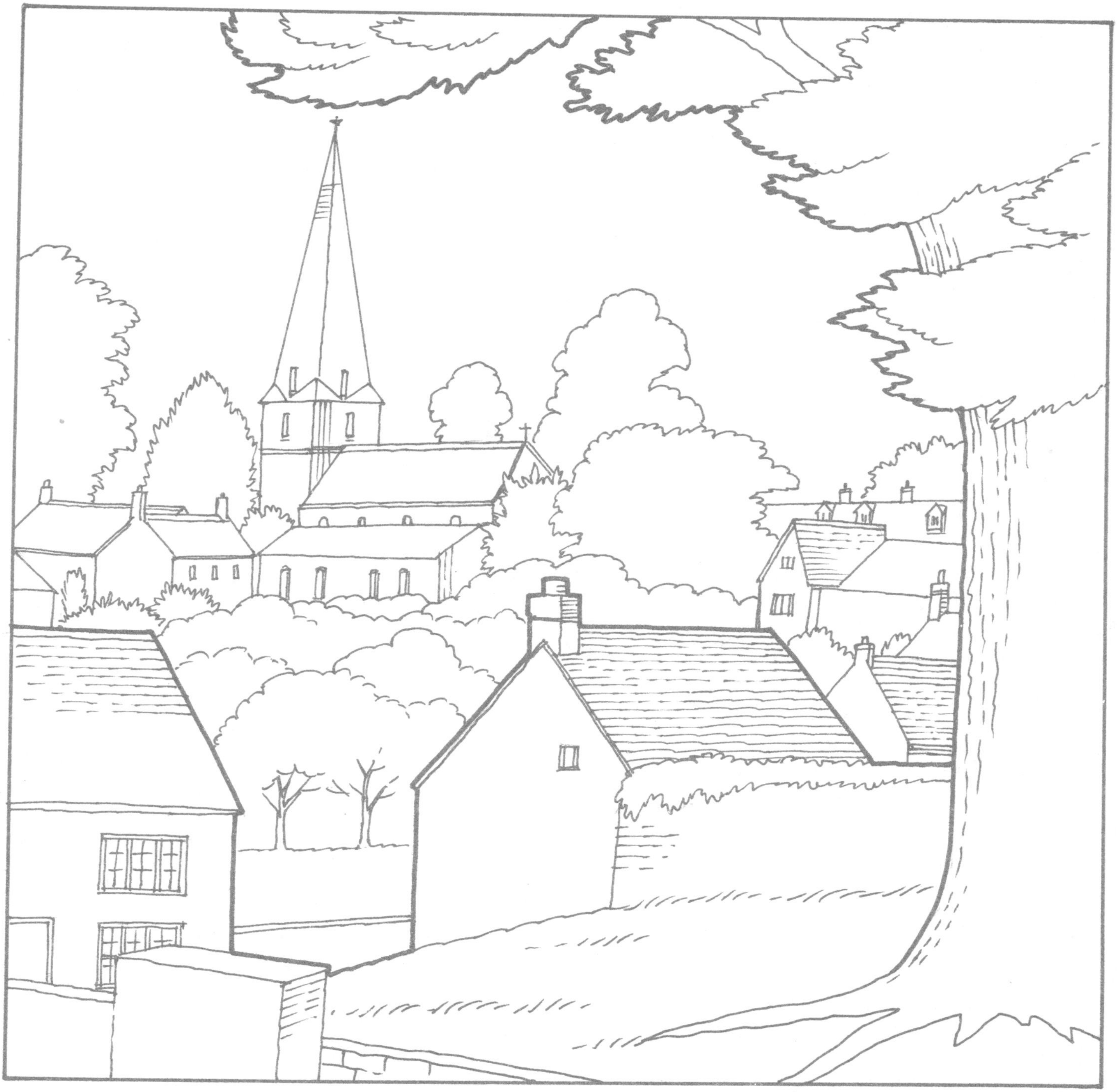

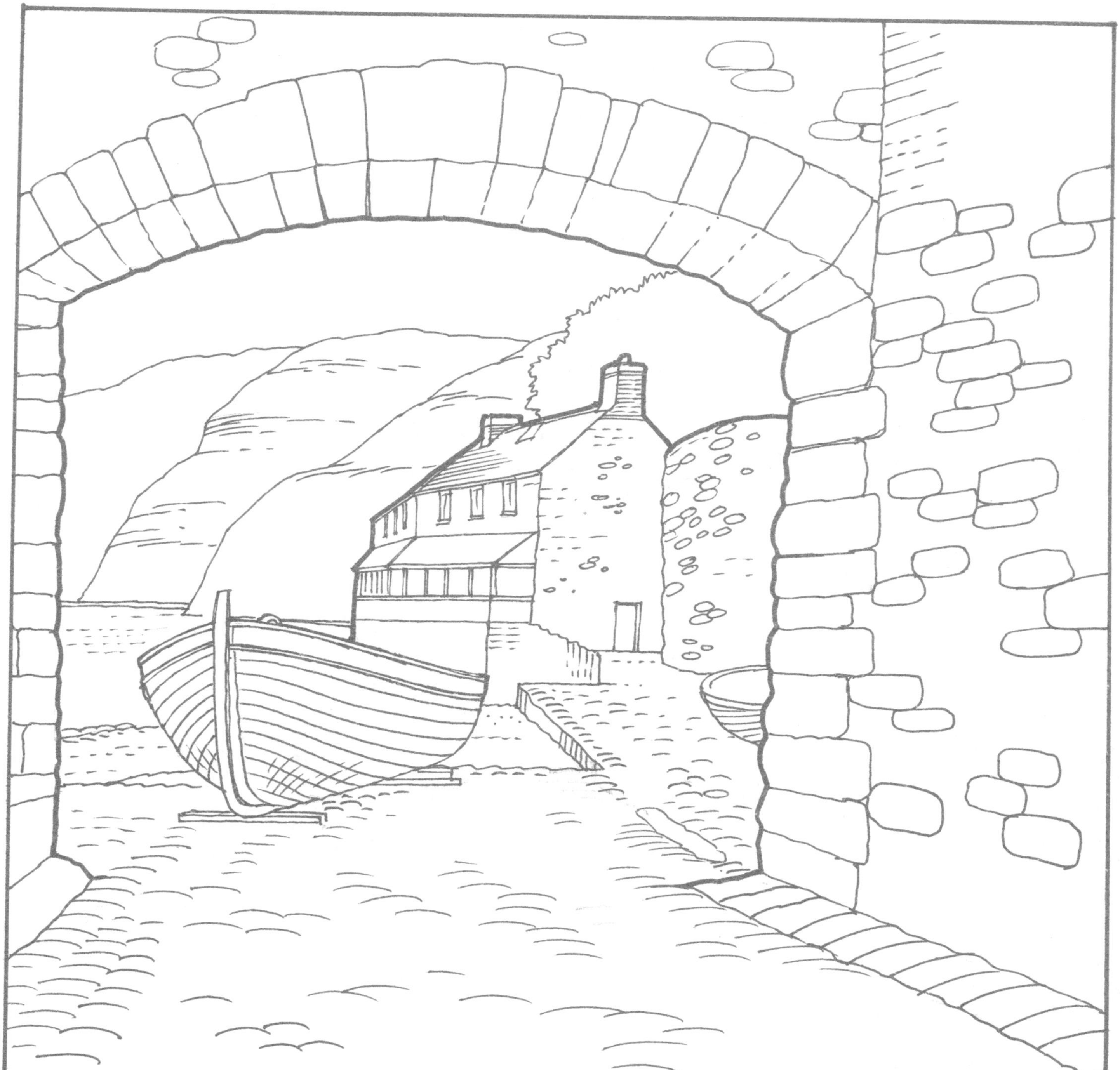

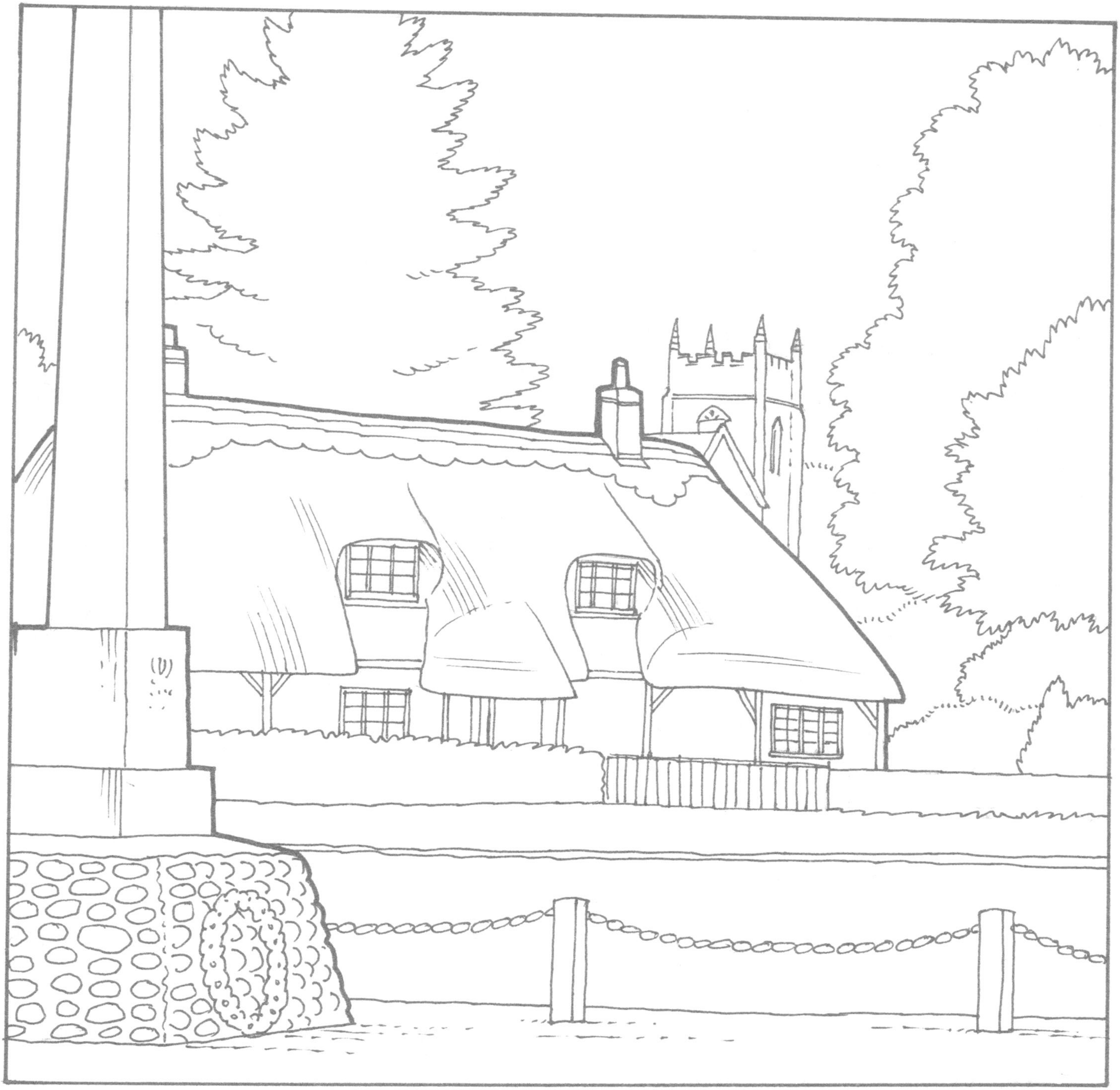

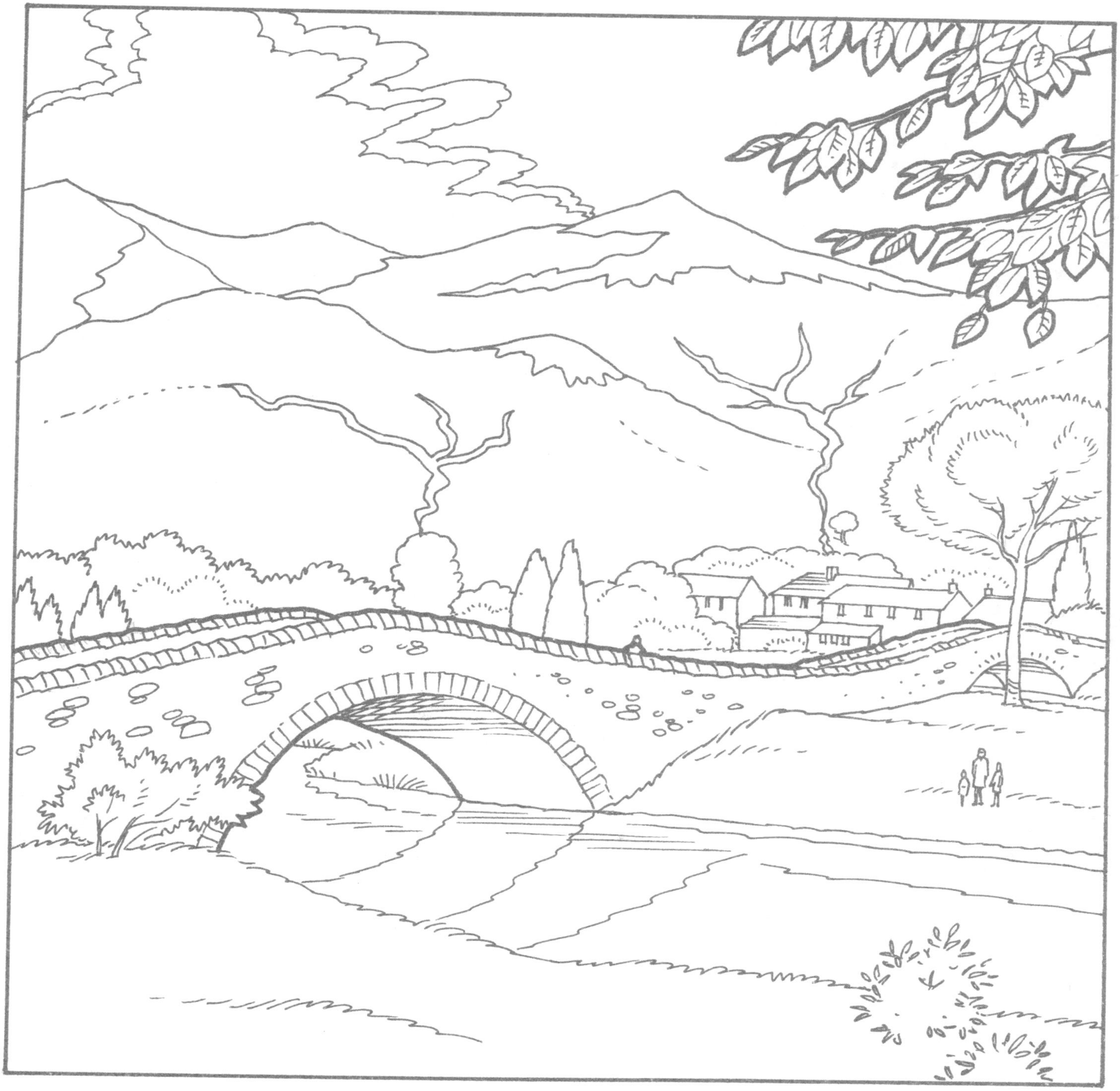

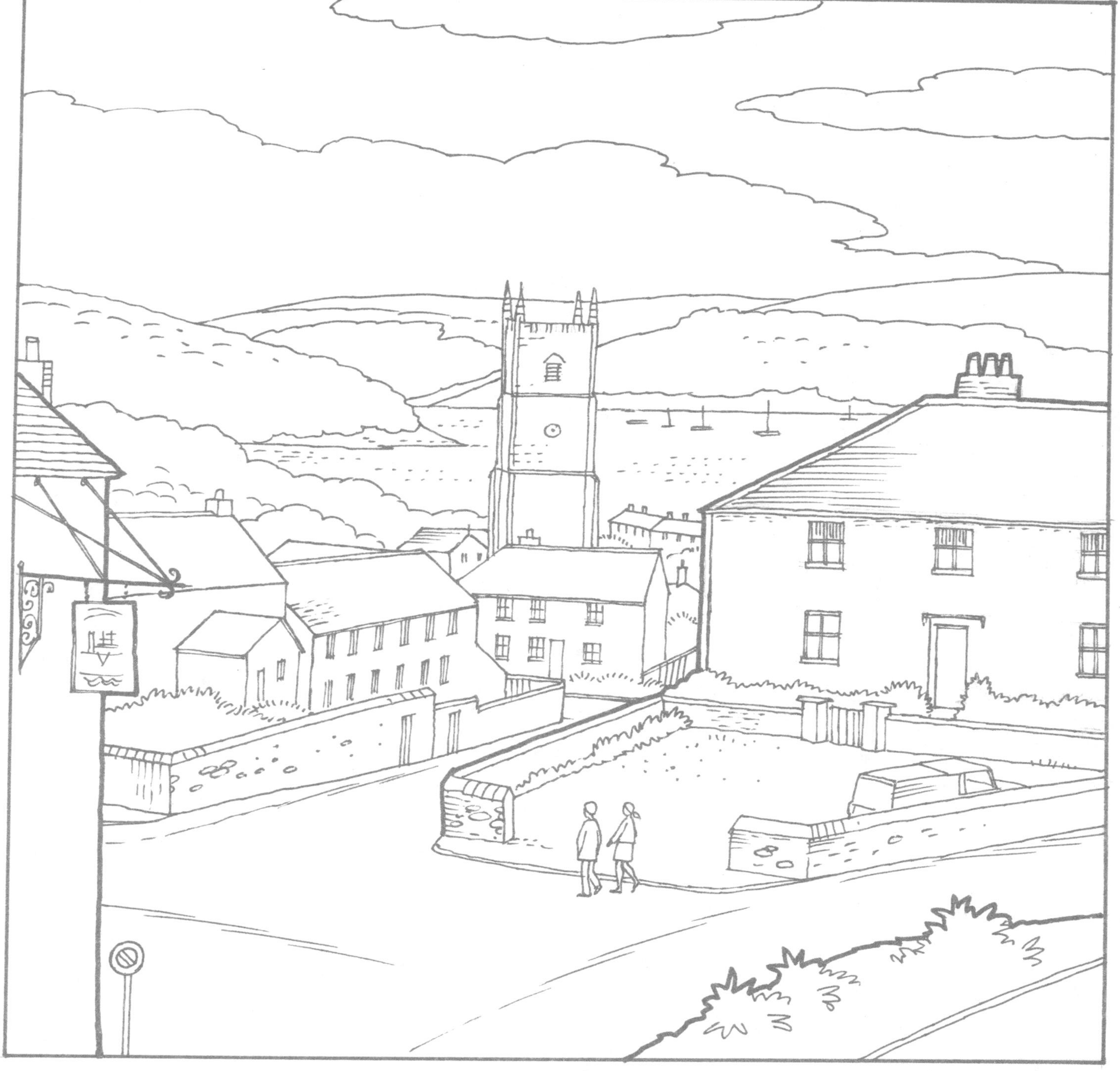

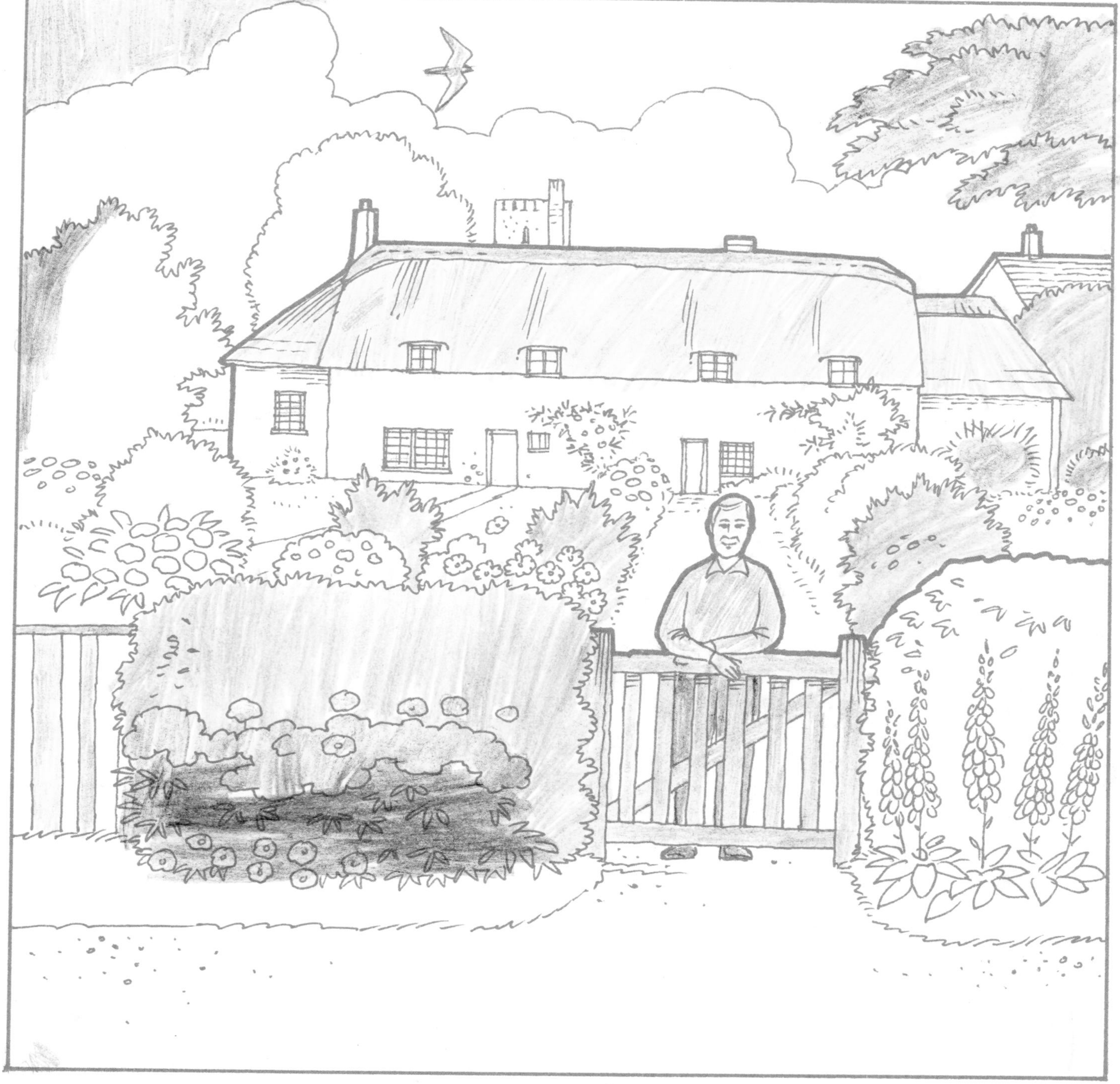

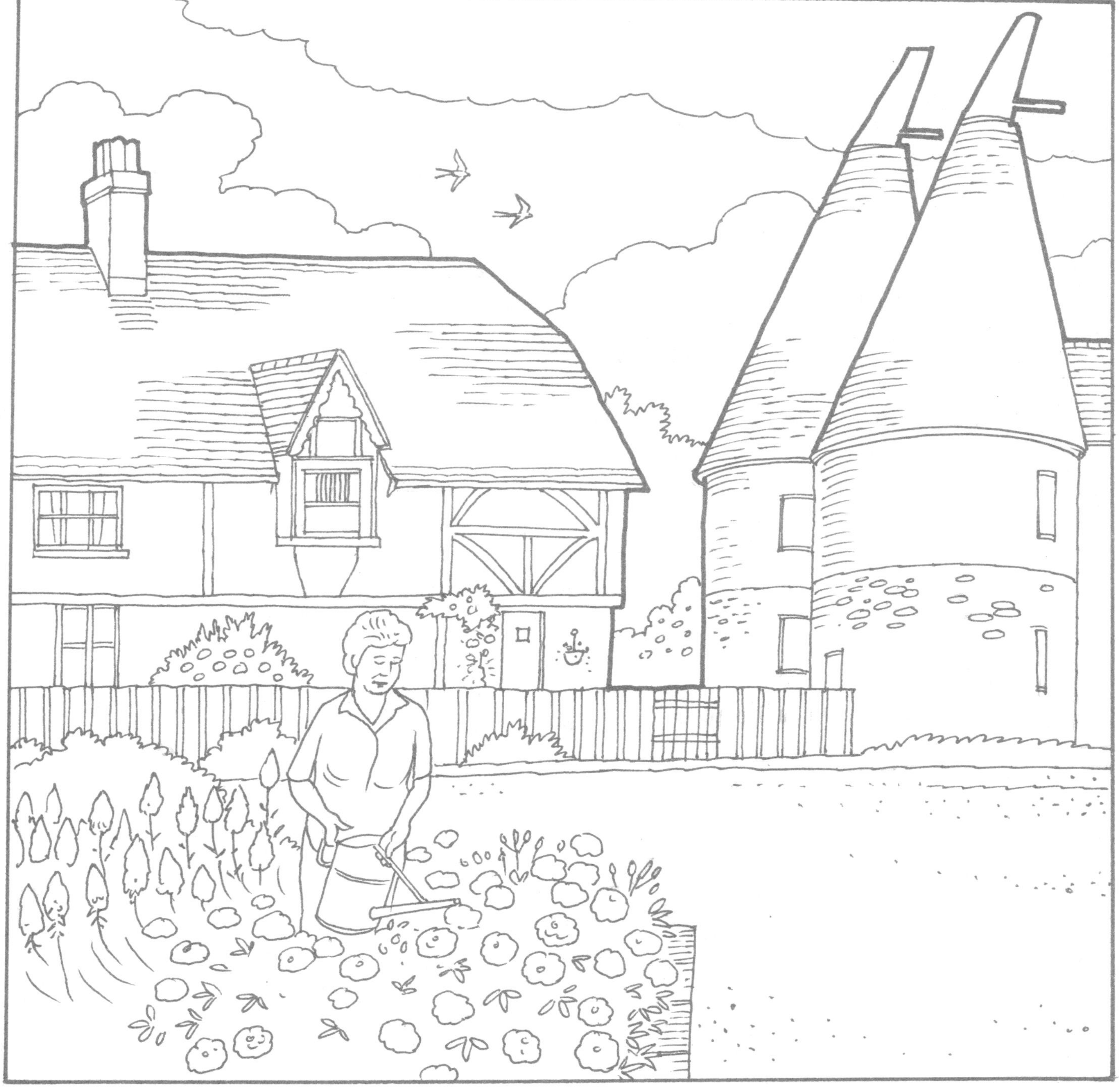

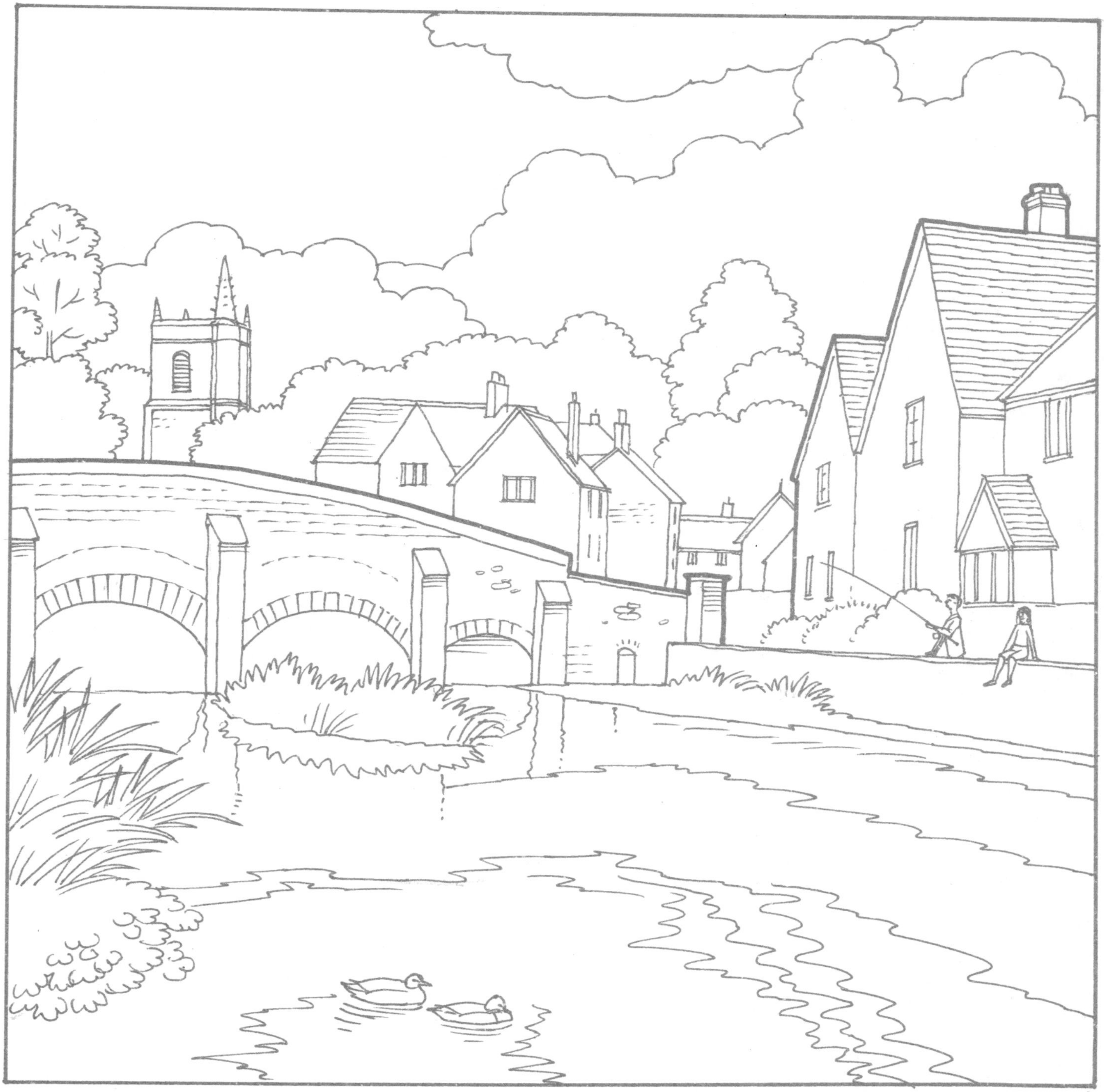